974.8
LAW

Lawton, Val

New York

3488000821129

NEW YORK

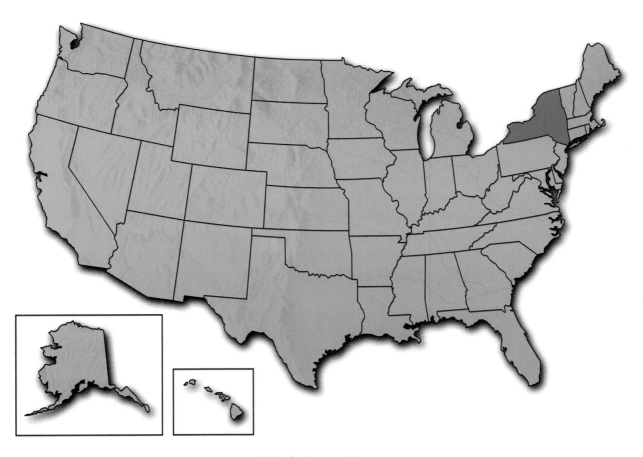

Val Lawton

Published by Weigl Publishers Inc.
123 South Broad Street, Box 227
Mankato, MN   56002
USA
Web site: http://www.weigl.com

Library of Congress Cataloging-in-Publication Data available upon request from the publisher. Fax: (507) 388-2746 for the attention of the Publishing Records Department.

ISBN 1-930954-49-2

Printed in the United States of America
1 2 3 4 5 6 7 8 9 10   05 04 03 02 01

Editor
Jennifer Nault
Substantive Editor
Jill Foran
Copy Editor
Kara Turner
Designers
Warren Clark
Terry Paulhus
Photo Researcher
Nicole Bezic King

Photograph Credits
Every reasonable effort has been made to trace ownership and to obtain permission to reprint copyright material. The publishers would be pleased to have any errors or omissions brought to their attention so that they may be corrected in subsequent printings.

Cover: fireworks over New York City (Corel Corporation), Statue of Liberty (Comstock Images); **Comstock Images:** pages 3B, 4BR, 6, 7T, 13B, 15B, 19BL, 20B, 21, 22T, 22BL, 24B, 29L; **Corbis Bettmann/Magma:** pages 7B, 17T, 18B, 19BR; **Corel Corporation:** pages 3T, 3M, 5T, 9, 11, 12B, 13T, 14B, 15T, 18T, 23T, 24T, 25T, 26B, 27B, 28T; **Hulton Getty/Stone:** page 17B; **NYS Department of Economic Development:** pages 4BL, 5B, 8B, 20T, 22BR, 26T, 27T, 28B, 29R; **PhotoDisc Inc:** pages 14T, 26M, 27B, **Photofest:** page 25B; **Steve Mulligan Photography:** pages 4T, 8T, 10, 12T, 23B; **Marilyn "Angel" Wynn:** page 16.

CONTENTS

At 7,540 square miles, Lake Ontario is one of the largest lakes in New York.

QUICK FACTS

The state of New York covers a total area of 54,475 square miles, making it the twenty-seventh largest state in the country.

In terms of area, New York City is the largest city in the state of New York. It is also the largest city in the United States, with a **metropolitan area** of 1,148 square miles.

New York's state motto is *Excelsior,* which means "ever upward."

INTRODUCTION

"I want to be a part of it, New York, New York!" This memorable line from the song "New York, New York" was sung by crooner Frank Sinatra. Today, these words still ring true, for if any state in the nation can have it all, it must be New York State. Situated in the northwestern United States, New York is home to a wide variety of breathtaking landscapes, fascinating cultures, and thriving communities. From its sandy beaches and rugged mountains to the hustle and bustle of New York City, the state of New York is a place of sharp contrasts.

New York State is nicknamed "The Empire State." This name is said to have originated in 1784, when George Washington toured New York's harbors and rich interior lands. Washington referred to New York as "The Seat of the Empire." Since then, the people of New York have worked hard to live up to their state's nickname. As a result, the Empire State is a national leader in manufacturing, finance, education, and the arts.

There are 578 miles of waterfront in New York City.

Since much of New York City is on Manhattan Island, bridges, such as the Brooklyn and Williamsburg Bridges, provide important links for commuters.

The Triborough Bridge, in New York City, is actually three bridges that connect Manhattan, Queens, and the Bronx.

New York is home to one of the world's longest suspension bridges. Called the Verrazano-Narrows Bridge, this suspension bridge connects Staten Island and Brooklyn, two of New York City's **boroughs**.

Getting There

The state of New York shares its northern borders with the Canadian provinces of Ontario and Quebec. Lake Ontario and Lake Erie border the state to the northwest and west, and Pennsylvania lies to the west and south of New York. Also to the south of New York are New Jersey and the Atlantic Ocean. New York shares its eastern borders with Connecticut, Massachusetts, and Vermont.

There are many ways to get to the Empire State. With nearly 500 airports, visitors can reach their destinations with ease. The three largest airports that serve the state are John F. Kennedy International Airport, LaGuardia, and Newark International Airport—which is actually in the nearby state of New Jersey. Together, these airports serve about 90 million passengers and handle more than 2.9 million tons of cargo every year. For those who prefer to travel by car, New York has about 110,000 miles of roads and highways. Trains also service parts of the state, and they play an important role in transporting commuters from New York City to surrounding areas.

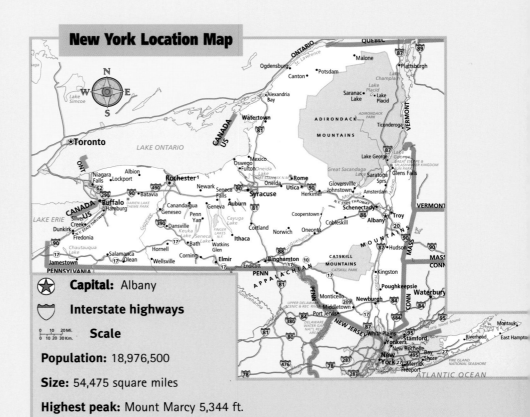

New York Location Map

★ **Capital:** Albany

Interstate highways

Scale 0 10 20 MI. / 0 10 20 30 Km.

Population: 18,976,500

Size: 54,475 square miles

Highest peak: Mount Marcy 5,344 ft.

New York's Statue of Liberty was a gift from France. It was given to the United States in 1884.

QUICK FACTS

Albany, situated on the west bank of the Hudson River in the east, is the capital of New York.

New York City served as the capital of the United States from 1785 to 1790. In 1789, the city's Federal Hall was the site of George Washington's **inauguration** as the country's first president.

The first railroad in the United States ran between Albany and Schenectady for a distance of 11 miles.

New York's Statue of Liberty, a gift from France, was packed in 214 wooden crates and shipped to the United States.

The Statue of Liberty's index finger measures 8 feet in length!

New York has a rich and exciting history. First occupied by Native Peoples more than 10,000 years ago, the New York region was established as a Dutch colony in 1624. Immigrants from many different European countries settled in the colony, which was then known as New Netherland. In 1664, England took over New Netherland and renamed the colony after the duke of York. New York remained an English colony for more than 100 years. Then, in 1775, New Yorkers joined neighboring colonies in the fight for American independence. After the signing of the Declaration of Independence, the people of New York held a convention to form their own constitution. It was adopted on April 20, 1777. On July 26, 1788, New York became the eleventh state to join the newly formed United States.

As part of the United States, New York continued to grow and prosper. By the early 1800s, it had become the most populous state in the nation. Immigrants from Europe continued to settle in New York, and developments in transportation and industry soon made the state one of the most powerful in the country. In 1946, New York City was selected as the permanent home of the United Nations. This move recognized New York City as a guardian of freedom and democracy.

A sculpture in the shape of a giant globe stands on the site of the United Nations headquarters.

Remembering September 11, 2001

On September 11, 2001, the world watched in horror as terrorists attacked the United States. At 8:45 AM, hijackers flew American Airlines Flight 11 into the north tower of New York City's World Trade Center. Located at the southern end of Manhattan Island, the World Trade Center's twin 110-story towers were considered the financial heart of the country. The airplane crashed through the building's exterior and set its upper floors on fire. Many people fled the tower as falling debris littered the area. Others were trapped inside. Eighteen minutes after the first crash, a second hijacked airplane, United Airlines Flight 175, hit the south tower of the World Trade Center and exploded. Within two hours of the crashes, the twin towers had collapsed. In total, more than 5,000 people were killed in the attacks, and thousands more were injured. This tragic event was the largest bloodshed on American soil since the Civil War.

Meanwhile, related tragedies were occurring elsewhere in the country. A third hijacked commercial airplane crashed into the Pentagon building in Washington, D.C., and a fourth passenger airplane crashed just outside Pittsburgh, Pennsylvania, killing many more people.

The events of September 11, 2001, had profound effects on New York, the rest of the country, and the entire world. On October 7, 2001, after gathering intelligence and international support, the United States and its allies began air strikes against terrorist camps in Afghanistan as part of the war on terrorism.

Heroism

The events of September 11, 2001, sparked many acts of heroism. While the twin towers of the World Trade Center burned and twisted under the effects of the plane crashes, people carried wounded strangers down many flights of stairs, putting their own lives at risk. People in the streets also tried to help, tearing off pieces of their clothing to use as bandages for the injured. Many firefighters and rescue workers rushed into the burning towers to save the thousands of people still trapped inside. Tragically, 343 firefighters lost their lives when the twin towers collapsed. Everyday activities in New York came to a halt in an effort to help those in need and ensure that others were kept safe. Buildings were evacuated, tunnels and bridges were closed, and airplanes were grounded all over the world. Despite the tragedies of the day, the people of New York City, under the leadership of Mayor Rudolph Giuliani, showed the world their tremendous courage and strength.

In New York City, a fireman raises the American flag.

Located in the Finger Lakes region in the rugged Appalachian Plateau, Watkins Glen Park boasts steep cliffs and nineteen waterfalls.

QUICK FACTS

Long Island is 118 miles long and measures only 23 miles at its widest point.

The state's major rivers include the Mohawk, the Hudson, the Oswego, the Genesee, the Seneca, the Delaware, and the Allegheny.

Thousands of years ago, glaciers covered the state and eroded the land. This carved out about 8,000 lakes that are found in New York.

The highest point in New York State is Mount Marcy, in the Adirondacks, which rises 5,344 feet.

New York had a record high temperature of 108°F in Troy on July 22, 1926. The lowest temperature in the state was –52°F at the Fulton Chain Lakes area on February 18, 1979.

LAND AND CLIMATE

The state of New York is made up of eight major land areas. In the north is the St. Lawrence Lowland, which runs along the banks of the St. Lawrence River. The forested Adirondack Upland is in the northeast. This area is home to the Adirondack Mountains. The Great Lakes Lowland region lines the shores of Lake Ontario and Lake Erie. The Hudson-Mohawk Lowland region covers the valleys of the Hudson and Mohawk Rivers. This region has some of the state's richest soils for farmland. The New England Upland region, which includes the heavily populated Manhattan Island, lies along the eastern state border, where the Taconic Mountains are found. The Atlantic Coastal Plain makes up Long Island and Staten Island. Lastly, the Appalachian Plateau and the Tug Hill Plateau cover most of southern New York and include the Catskill Mountains.

New York's climate varies greatly. For instance, the average January temperature ranges from 14° Fahrenheit in the central Adirondacks to 30°F on Long Island. Much of upstate New York experiences long, cold winters.

The Catskill Mountain chain is approximately 70 miles long and 50 miles wide. The tallest peak in the Catskills is Slide Mountain, which stands at over 4,200 feet.

NATURAL RESOURCES

There is commercial and recreational fishing in the lower Great Lakes and in the Atlantic Ocean.

One of New York's most important natural resources is water. There are more than 8,000 lakes and many significant rivers in the state. Some of New York's rivers are used to provide **hydroelectric power**. In fact, the dam at Niagara Falls, located on the New York–Ontario border, is one of the largest producers of hydroelectricity in the world. The state's waters also support a lucrative commercial fishing industry. Catches off the Atlantic coast include clams, oysters, and scallops, while a variety of freshwater fish are pulled from Lakes Erie and Ontario.

The state's mining industry supplies crushed stone, cement, sand, and gravel—all of which are used in construction. As well, New York is a large supplier of salt. The state is just about the only place in the world where a mineral called anorthosite is mined. Anorthosite is a durable rock that is very common on the moon but quite rare on Earth. New York's Mount Marcy and Whiteface Mountain are composed mainly of anorthosite.

Much of New York's cement production takes place in the Hudson River Valley, in upstate New York.

PLANTS AND ANIMALS

New York was once almost entirely forested. As people settled in the area, many of these forests were cleared for farmland, or to build cities and towns. Today, forests cover about 60 percent of New York's land area, and they feature a rich mixture of **deciduous** and **coniferous** species. Among the many types of softwoods found in New York's forests are white pines, spruces, and hemlocks. Hardwoods in the state include beeches, oaks, and yellow birches. New York's official state tree, the sugar maple, grows in many parts of the state. Native to the northern United States, the sugar maple produces sap that is tapped, collected, and boiled to make delicious maple syrup.

A variety of wild plants and flowers also grow throughout New York. About 1,900 species of plants are native to the state. Flowering plants found in New York's forests include violets, bellworts, and hepaticas. In the spring, wildflowers such as buttercups, daisies, and asters decorate the state's meadows and hillsides.

At Adirondack Park, leaves, such as those on the smooth sumac, turn a variety of colors in the fall.

QUICK FACTS

More than fifty-eight species of wild orchids grow in New York.

Apple trees were first planted in New York in the 1600s, with the arrival of European settlers who brought seeds from their homelands.

New York has 163 state parks and 700,000 acres of forest preserves.

In 1891, schoolchildren across the state voted for the official flower of New York—the rose.

Nearly half of Adirondack Park, the nation's largest state park, will remain wild forever, thanks to a state law written in 1892.

Tourists visit the state just to see New York's colorful fall foliage.

New York is home to a large variety of wildlife. Black bears forage in the mountain areas, while white-tailed deer and smaller mammals, such as beavers, foxes, minks, opossums, and raccoons, inhabit the forests. Unfortunately, some mammals including the cougar and timber wolf are endangered in New York's woodlands. Many of these animals have been subject to overhunting, while others have had their natural habitats threatened by logging or land development. Today, various wildlife management programs work to re-establish certain animal populations.

Black bears are not always black—they can be brown, cinnamon, or even white in color.

New York's waters are host to an abundance of aquatic life. Many different species of freshwater fish are found in the state's lakes and rivers. These fish include bass, perch, pickerel, and trout. In the ocean, tuna, bass, flounder, and different kinds of shellfish may be found. The state's coastal waters also provide habitat for whales, dolphins, and seals.

There are many raccoons in New York's wilderness areas. Raccoons do not have rings around their eyes and tails until about ten days after they are born.

Approximately 10 million people visit the Niagara Reservation State Park every year.

QUICK FACTS

New York City's Central Park draws tourists year-round. First opened in 1859, the park was the first landscaped public park in the United States.

Tarrytown, just north of New York City, was settled by the Dutch in the seventeenth century. Today, it remains a popular tourist draw. People come to see Sleepy Hollow, where the fictional Ichabod Crane was chased by the Headless Horseman. The tale "The Legend of Sleepy Hollow" was written by Washington Irving.

A piece of New York State history can be experienced at the Old Dutch Reformed Church in Tarrytown. Now restored, it is a national historic landmark. The graves of Washington Irving, Andrew Carnegie, and William Rockefeller are also found in Tarrytown.

TOURISM

New York State is one of the most popular destinations for travelers to the United States. Approximately 17 million tourists travel to New York State every year, making it the third most-visited state in the nation. Some people come to see the bright lights of Manhattan, while other visitors wish to enjoy the vast wilderness of the Adirondacks. Some visit the state to lounge on the beaches of Long Island, while others head to Chautauqua County for the area's excellent bird-watching opportunities.

One of the state's greatest tourist draws is the world-renowned Niagara Falls. These impressive falls are a popular honeymoon destination for newlyweds. On the New York side, the falls are called the American Falls, and they cascade from a height of about 180 feet. Visitors can travel beneath the falls aboard *The Maid of the Mist*, a steamboat that has been in operation since 1846. Those aboard *The Maid of the Mist* are able to experience the falls at such close proximity that they require rain gear.

Home to one of the world's most vibrant theater districts, Manhattan's Broadway attracts theatergoers from around the globe.

New York's wines, considered to be among the best in the United States, are produced mainly in the Finger Lakes region and around Lake Erie.

INDUSTRY

New York manufactures more goods than almost any other state in the country—only California has a larger manufacturing output. With about 26,000 industrial plants, the state produces many different kinds of goods. Books, magazines, newspapers, and other printed materials are important factory items. In fact, New York publishes more printed matter than any other state in the country. The largest portion of publishing activity takes place in the New York City area, which contributes 10 percent of the national output.

Other manufacturing centers in the state produce electrical and medical equipment, computer equipment, clothing, plastics, and chemicals, which include **pharmaceuticals**. For instance, Bristol-Myers Squibb, a major pharmaceutical company, is headquartered in New York City. Chemicals rank first among New York's manufactured products.

Street vendors display an array of reading materials, many of which have been published in New York City.

QUICK FACTS

The value of New York's manufactured goods makes up about 7 percent of the country's total production.

Most of the food processed in New York is grown and harvested in the state. New York has about 38,000 farms. More than half of the state's farm income is obtained from the production of milk and milk products.

Significant fruit and vegetable crops are harvested in the state, and New York is a leader in the production of apples, grapes, and potatoes.

Only California and Washington produce more grapes for wine than New York does.

New York has a highly respected fashion industry. Many clothing design houses, such as Calvin Klein, are based in New York City.

GOODS AND SERVICES

New York is an industrial powerhouse. The state provides the nation with a variety of goods, from fresh fruit to fashionable clothing to state-of-the-art electrical equipment. Many of New York's goods are **exported** to other states and countries. The state's excellent transportation system makes it a leader in distribution. Busy port facilities in places such as New York City, Buffalo, and Albany handle many of these goods.

One of the most historically significant transportation systems in New York was the Erie Canal. Opened in 1825, it connected the Atlantic Ocean with the Great Lakes. The canal produced great revenues for the state and helped to settle the Midwest. In 1918, the New York State Barge Canal was opened to replace the Erie Canal. This system incorporates parts of the Erie Canal and supports much water traffic. It is the shortest route from the Atlantic Ocean to the Great Lakes.

New York's waterways are busy with recreational boats and cargo ships. About 19 million metric tons of cargo pass through the port each year.

The New York Stock Exchange lists more major corporations than any other stock exchange in the nation.

If New York State were a country, its economy would rank among the world's top fifteen.

New York's earliest newspaper, *The New-York Gazette*, was first published in 1725. Today, more than eighty daily newspapers are published in the state.

New York City serves as the headquarters for three major television networks. They are the National Broadcasting Company (NBC), the Columbia Broadcasting System (CBS), and the American Broadcasting Company (ABC).

New York is the center of commerce and finance in the United States. Many of the country's leading businesses and financial institutions have their head offices in New York City. The city's financial district, which is centered on Manhattan's Wall Street, is home to some of the world's most powerful banks, brokerages, and stock exchanges. The New York Stock Exchange (NYSE) is a driving force in the nation's economy. The NYSE's origins can be traced back to 1792, when twenty-four New York City stockbrokers and merchants came together for trading purposes. Today, it is the world's largest and most influential securities marketplace.

New York is also a center for higher education. The state has 88 public and 226 private post-secondary institutions. In 1948, the State University of New York (SUNY) was established to supervise all tax-supported universities. SUNY comprises sixty-four schools throughout the state. Other places of higher learning in the state include New York University, Columbia University, Cornell University, Syracuse University, and Vassar College. The University of Rochester, as well as the Juilliard School and the Manhattan School of Music, are all known for their excellent music programs.

New York City is home to the world's most extensive subway system.

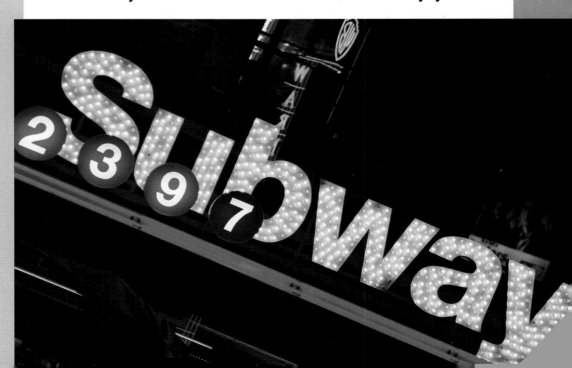

FIRST NATIONS

People have lived in the New York region for more than 10,000 years. Native Peoples were the first to inhabit the area. **Archeological** evidence suggests that more than 8,000 early Native Peoples lived along the banks of the lower Hudson River and on Staten, Long, and Manhattan islands. By the late sixteenth century, two major Native-American groups—the Algonquin and the Iroquois Confederacy— inhabited much of New York. The Algonquin consisted of many smaller groups, including the Delaware, Mohican, Montauk, Munsee, and Wappinger. These groups lived chiefly in the Hudson Valley and on Long Island. They grew corn, beans, and squash, but also hunted, trapped, and fished. Algonquin groups built and lived in long wooden structures called longhouses. These structures were often home to more than fifty people.

Like the Algonquin, the Iroquois established farming communities and lived in longhouses. Each Iroquois community was run by a ruling council and a village chief, while the entire Confederacy was run by a council of delegates.

Despite signing a treaty of friendship with English settlers in 1682, the Delaware were gradually pushed west.

QUICK FACTS

The Iroquois were very powerful, and they often fought with the neighboring Algonquin and amongst themselves. In 1570, five Iroquois groups living in the New York region established peace among their groups when they formed the Iroquois Confederacy.

The Iroquois Confederacy was known as the Five Nations until the early 1700s, when the Tuscarora joined and the Confederacy became known as the Six Nations.

The name *Manhattan* is an Algonquian word meaning "hilly island."

Some historians believe that the Iroquois Confederacy of 1570 influenced and helped to create the United States Constitution.

The Verrazano-Narrows Bridge in New York City is named after Giovanni da Verrazano.

EXPLORERS AND MISSIONARIES

The first European to reach New York was an Italian navigator named Giovanni da Verrazano. Hired by the King of France to explore North America, Verrazano sailed into New York Harbor in 1524. He left, however, without exploring the region. Two years later, a Spanish adventurer also came upon New York Harbor, but, like Verrazano, he did not explore the area.

It was not until 1609 that a European actually surveyed the New York region. That year, an Englishman named Henry Hudson reached the mouth of the Hudson River on a ship called the *Half Moon*. Employed by the Dutch East Indian Company, Hudson was assigned to find the Northwest Passage, a sea route that would provide a shortcut to Asia. Although he did not find the Northwest Passage, Hudson wrote a report describing the area of New York. This report generated interest from his employers in the Netherlands, and soon the Dutch had claimed much of the New York region. The Dutch named the area New Netherland and began building permanent settlements.

Henry Hudson and his crew met many Native Americans during the month they spent exploring the Hudson River.

EARLY SETTLERS

St. Patrick's Cathedral was built to replace the original cathedral, which dated back to 1879.

New Netherland's first European settlers were sent by the Dutch West India Company in 1624. The company sent more than 100 women, men, and children to settle the new colony. Most of the settlers were French Huguenots—Protestants who were fleeing religious **persecution** in France. They immigrated to New Netherland so that they would be free to worship as they pleased. The Huguenots established the colony's first settlement, Fort Orange, in the northern Hudson Valley. One year later, more colonists established a settlement on the southern tip of Manhattan Island, naming it New Amsterdam.

The settlements of New Netherland grew slowly at first. In order to help increase settlement numbers, the Dutch West India Company offered large tracts of land to its members in 1629. Members were informed that they could keep the land if they were able to bring fifty settlers to the colony within four years. Owners of the tracts rented land plots and farmland to tenants. Many people came to the colony to farm. New Netherland, unlike other colonies in North America, tolerated all nationalities and religions. As a result, people from many different religious and ethnic groups moved there.

QUICK FACTS

For many years, the French Huguenots had been forced to worship secretly because they were **dissenters** from the Church of Rome. The word *hugeon* means "house worshipper."

In 1647, Peter Stuyvesant was named governor of New Netherland. Under his leadership, New Netherland began to prosper.

In the 1650s, many Jewish people who were fleeing persecution in Eastern Europe and Russia settled in New Netherland.

Under Peter Stuyvesant's leadership, the settlement of New Amsterdam established a city council, and protective walls were erected.

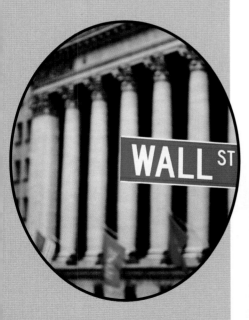

By the late 1600s, New Netherland was beginning to grow. Immigrants from countries such as France, Germany, Denmark, Poland, England, and Italy came to start new lives. These settlers all contributed to the cultural and economic growth of the colony. However, it was the Dutch who held the greatest influence, creating services such as the state's first police force and fire brigade.

The Dutch ruled New Netherland until 1664. That year, England took over the area. New Netherland had always been a source of frustration for England. Colonies belonging to England surrounded New Netherland on the south and north. The position of these colonies along the Atlantic coast meant that England could control shipping through its ports. However, many traders were able to bypass England's strict shipping rules by sailing in and out of New Amsterdam's harbor. King Charles II of England decided to end this activity by taking over the region. He granted all of the land between the Connecticut and Delaware Rivers to his brother James, Duke of York and Albany. To enforce this claim, the duke sent four warships to New Amsterdam's harbor. The people of New Amsterdam knew that they had no chance of winning a battle and quickly surrendered to the English. The colony was renamed New York.

Just three years after Peter Stuyvesant peacefully surrendered New Amsterdam to the English, the rest of New Netherland came under English control.

Since its early days as New Netherland, New York has attracted people of many different ethnic and religious backgrounds.

QUICK FACTS

It is estimated that one in three people living in the United States today has a close relative who came through Ellis Island's immigrant processing center.

Because of its historical importance, Ellis Island was made part of the Statue of Liberty National Monument in 1965.

About 9 percent of New York City dwellers are Jewish.

Nearly 16 percent of New Yorkers were born outside of the United States.

New York's second-largest city is Buffalo, with about 330,000 residents.

The most densely populated area in New York is King's County, or Brooklyn. There are 2.4 million residents living within an area of 71 square miles.

POPULATION

Between the years 1892 and 1954, more than 12 million immigrants passed through the immigration processing center on Ellis Island and arrived in the port of New York.

Today, New York has a population of about 19 million. This represents nearly 7 percent of the nation's total population. Only California has more residents than New York. Although it is not the most populous state, New York is home to the nation's most populated city. New York City has a population of 8.7 million people. The city consists of five boroughs—Manhattan, Brooklyn, the Bronx, Queens, and Staten Island. Manhattan, the smallest of these boroughs, has about 1.5 million people.

New York is one of the most densely populated states in the country. Compared to the national average of 80 people per square mile, New York State has 402 people per square mile.

No longer used as an immigration processing center, Ellis Island became a museum in 1990. It stores documents related to 400 years of immigration history in the United States.

New York has served as the headquarters of the United Nations since 1952. The United Nations has its own security forces and fire and postal departments.

QUICK FACTS

New York State is divided into fifty-seven counties. Each county has a board of supervisors that governs on a local level.

New York became the eleventh state on July 26, 1788.

The United States Constitution was ratified in 1788.

New York's constitution of 1894 has been amended more than 180 times.

By the end of the 1990s, the mayor of New York City was Rudolph Giuliani. He was born and raised in Brooklyn. Giuliani ran successfully for mayor of the nation's largest city in 1993 and was re-elected in 1997. He has been credited with lowering the crime rate in the city by 57 percent.

POLITICS AND GOVERNMENT

New York was the first of the thirteen colonies to draft its constitution, which was completed in 1777. This constitution was also the first to assert that the governor must be elected by the people of the state, rather than be appointed by a state official.

New York's state government is divided into three branches—executive, legislative, and judicial. The governor of New York is the head of the executive branch. He or she serves a term of 4 years. The governor is responsible for proposing the state budget, appointing state department directors, and for signing bills into laws. New York's legislative branch makes the state laws. It is composed of a 61-member senate and a 150-member assembly. Voters from each district elect senate and assembly members to 2-year terms. The judicial branch interprets and enforces the state's laws.

Officially called "Liberty Enlightening the World," New York's Statue of Liberty is a symbol of democracy.

CULTURAL GROUPS

New York is home to a broad range of cultural groups. Throughout the state's history, immigrants from many different countries have chosen to make their home in New York. In the seventeenth century, when the Dutch colony of New Amsterdam had reached 1,000 people, there were fifteen different languages spoken on Manhattan Island.

Throughout the eighteenth and nineteenth centuries, the largest groups of immigrants arrived in New York from Russia, Poland, Ireland, Austria, Canada, and England. There were also great numbers of people arriving from Italy, Germany, and Romania. People left their homelands for different reasons. Some were fleeing religious persecution or famine, while others were simply looking for new opportunities. Many of the immigrants who passed through the gates at Ellis Island chose to remain in New York City. As a result, it is the most multicultural city in the United States. Today, there are more people of Italian descent living in New York City than in Naples, Italy, and more people of Irish descent than live in Dublin, Ireland.

As many as 150,000 people live in New York City's Chinatown, making it the largest Chinatown in the United States.

QUICK FACTS

Nearly 60 percent of New Yorkers are of European heritage, while just less than 16 percent are of African-American heritage.

In the early 1900s, many African Americans seeking better working and social conditions came to New York. Today, the state's largest African-American community is located in Brooklyn. More than 40 percent of the residents in Brooklyn are African American.

The San Gennaro Festival is New York's largest street festival. Every September, more than 3 million people come to Little Italy during an 11-day period to honor Saint Januarius of Naples.

St. Patrick's Day festivities were first held in 1766 by Irish soldiers serving in the American colonies.

QUICK FACTS

The Oneida Nation is the largest employer in both Madison and Oneida counties. Among its many establishments are a resort hotel, campgrounds, a casino, and several retail stores.

The New York State Museum in Albany is the oldest state museum in the United States.

People of Scottish descent in New York celebrate their heritage with the New York Scottish Games. Held every year in Syracuse, this event features bagpipe music, Scottish food, Highland dancing, and traditional athletic competitions.

More than 82,000 Native Americans make their homes in New York. Many descendants of the Six Nations of the Iroquois Confederacy still live in the state. The largest of these groups is the Seneca Nation, and the second largest is the Mohawk. Three Seneca **reservations** are located in western New York, and the Mohawk have land in the northern part of the state. The Oneida Nation is also part of the Iroquois Confederacy. Today, people of the Oneida Nation live in central New York. New York's Native Americans celebrate their traditions with festivals and events, such as powwows, throughout the year.

Like the state's Native Americans, many of New York's other cultural groups honor and celebrate their own traditions. For example, Irish New Yorkers celebrate their heritage every March 17 in New York City. On this day, people of Irish descent gather together to celebrate St. Patrick's Day. They pay tribute to St. Patrick, the patron saint of Ireland, with a grand parade that sweeps through the streets of New York City.

Seneca Falls, New York, is known as the birthplace of women's rights. It is the site of the first women's rights convention in the nation.

ARTS AND ENTERTAINMENT

New York is a leading center for the arts. In the 1800s, the breathtaking scenery of the Hudson River Valley inspired artists such as Thomas Cole, to paint beautiful landscapes of the valley and the Catskill Mountains. Their style of painting became known as the Hudson River School. In the 1930s, New York artists developed a style known as **abstract expressionism**, and in the 1960s, New Yorkers Andy Warhol and Robert Rauschenberg were leaders in the creation of **pop art**. Today, visual artists across the state continue to create innovative artwork.

Manhattan's theater district is known as Broadway. Stage performers from around the world often dream of performing on Broadway. New York City is known for other artistic venues as well. For more than a century, Carnegie Hall has hosted many of the world's greatest musicians.

In addition to being one of New York City's most popular tourist attractions, The Met is also an important educational institution.

QUICK FACTS

The country's largest arts complex is the Lincoln Center for the Performing Arts. It is home to the Metropolitan Opera and the New York City Ballet.

The Lincoln Center is so large that it covers 16 acres of Manhattan.

The work of the Hudson River artists can be seen at the Albany Institute of History and Art.

The Metropolitan Museum of Art was established in Manhattan in 1870. Covering about 2 million square feet and housing more than 3 million pieces of art, "The Met" is considered the largest museum in the Western Hemisphere.

Archeologists and art historians conduct research at The Met, and a variety of lectures and educational programs are available to the public.

Tchaikovsky, Duke Ellington, Liza Minnelli, and the Beatles are among the many performers who have drawn crowds to Carnegie Hall.

New York City's theater district, with its many lights and billboards along Broadway and Times Square, is sometimes called "The Great White Way."

Some of the country's most celebrated writers and entertainers hail from the Empire State. Walt Whitman, often considered the nation's greatest poet, was born on Long Island in 1819. Other popular early writers from New York include Herman Melville, who wrote the great whaling adventure *Moby Dick*, and Washington Irving, a popular essayist and short-story writer. Irving based many of his stories on the Dutch legends of the Hudson River Valley. Among his best-loved tales are "Rip Van Winkle" and "The Legend of Sleepy Hollow." In the early twentieth century, New Yorker Edith Wharton wrote stories set in New York City. Her novel *The Age Of Innocence* won the Pulitzer Prize in 1921, making Wharton the first woman to ever receive the **prestigious** literary award. Playwrights from New York include Eugene O'Neill, Arthur Miller, and Neil Simon.

Actor and director Woody Allen, comedian Jerry Seinfeld, actor Christopher Reeve, and singer Barbra Streisand are all modern-day entertainers from New York City. Comedian Rosie O'Donnell is from Commack, singer Billy Joel was born in Hicksville, and movie star Tom Cruise was born in Syracuse.

QUICK FACTS

On Christmas Eve
of 1822, New York professor Clarke Moore wrote a poem for his children called *A Visit from St. Nicholas.* Today, this poem is known as *The Night Before Christmas,* and it is one of the most widely read Christmas poems in the world.

The Marx Brothers
were a family of comedians who became known in the 1930s for films such as *Animal Crackers, Monkey Business,* and *Duck Soup.* The brothers were from New York City.

Born Allen Stewart Konigsberg, Woody Allen has either directed, written, or starred in more than forty films. In 1977, he won an Academy Award for Best Director for the film *Annie Hall.*

SPORTS

Camping is a popular way to enjoy New York's beautiful and diverse landscape.

New York provides its residents and visitors with the opportunity to enjoy a variety of outdoor activities. In the warmer months, many outdoor enthusiasts flock to the state's mountains and forests to go hiking, camping, or mountain climbing. Water sports are also popular in the summer. Boating, fishing, and swimming are enjoyed at places such as Lake George, the Thousand Islands, and the Finger Lakes. The Hudson River offers great canoeing and white-water rafting trips, while sailing is a common activity off the Atlantic coast. In the winter, New York's snow-covered mountains provide great opportunities for skiing, snowboarding, and tobogganing, and its many wilderness trails are ideal for cross-country skiing and snowmobiling. Lake Placid, which hosted the Winter Olympics twice, offers excellent winter sports facilities, including some of the finest ski jumps in the world.

QUICK FACTS

Every summer, the best tennis players in the world travel to Flushing Meadows, Queens, to play in the U.S. Open.

Many of the world's top long-distance runners travel to New York every fall to compete in the challenging New York City Marathon.

When the New York City Marathon was first held in 1970, only 55 people finished the race. Today, the event attracts about 30,000 participants, as well as 12,000 volunteers, 2,000 police, and thousands of spectators.

The sport of lacrosse is a combination of basketball, soccer, and hockey.

The National Baseball Hall of Fame is located in Cooperstown.

New York is home to many professional sports teams. Hockey fans across the state cheer for the Buffalo Sabres, the New York Rangers, and the New York Islanders. All three teams are part of the National Hockey League. Football fans throughout the state also cheer for three professional teams—The Buffalo Bills, the New York Giants, and the New York Jets are all part of the National Football League. The New York Knicks are part of the National Basketball Association, and the New York Liberty are a team in the Women's National Basketball Association.

Perhaps the most popular team in the state is the New York Yankees. Based in New York City, the Yankees are one of the best-loved major league baseball teams in the country. Originally known as the New York Highlanders in the early 1900s, the team's name was changed to the Yankees in 1913. In 1920, a player named Babe Ruth joined the team. Ruth was one of the best hitters of all time. Every season, he hit an amazing number of home runs, and soon baseball fans across the country were cheering for Ruth and the Yankees as they won game after game. As time went on, several other Yankees players, including baseball heroes such as Lou Gehrig, Joe DiMaggio, and Mickey Mantle, drew national attention. Today, the Yankees remain one of the most successful sports teams in the world.

QUICK FACTS

The New York Yankees play their home games at Yankee Stadium, in the Bronx. This enormous stadium is commonly called "The House of Champions."

As well as cheering for the Yankees, major league baseball fans in New York also cheer for the New York Mets.

In 1845, a New Yorker named Alexander Cartwright played a key role in writing the official rules for the game of baseball.

Although they are considered New York football teams, the New York Jets and the New York Giants play their home games in the nearby state of New Jersey.

Baseball is often called the national pastime of the United States, because of its strong tradition and great popularity.

Brain Teasers

1

The Erie Canal ran between which two cities in New York?

Answer: It ran 363 miles from Albany by the Hudson River, to Buffalo by Lake Erie.

2

Why is the name "David Letterman" synonymous with New York City?

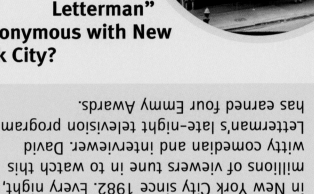

Answer: David Letterman has hosted a late-night television show based in New York City since 1982. Every night, millions of viewers tune in to watch this witty comedian and interviewer. David Letterman's late-night television program has earned four Emmy Awards.

3

TRUE OR FALSE?

The very first pizzeria in the United States was established in New York City.

Answer: True. Gennaro Lombardi opened the pizzeria in 1905.

4

TRUE OR FALSE?

The state flag bears the image of justice with a hand over her mouth.

Answer: False. The state flag bears the image of justice blindfolded, meaning that all people are entitled to equal treatment in the eyes of the law.

5 **A farmer's field just outside of Bethel, in New York's Catskills,** was the scene of which famous music festival in 1969?

a) The US Music Festival

b) Lilith Fair

c) The Woodstock Music and Arts Fair

d) The Monterey International Pop Festival

Answer: c. The Woodstock Music and Arts Fair

8 **Approximately what percent of the state's residents live in New York City?**

a) 25 percent

b) 45 percent

c) 75 percent

d) 90 percent

Answer: b. Forty-five percent.

7 **"Soho" is a district in New York City. What does the word stand for?**

Answer: Soho means "south of Houston."

6 **Who founded the United States Military Academy at West Point in 1802?**

Answer: Thomas Jefferson

FOR MORE INFORMATION

Books

Aylesworth, Thomas G. and Virginia L. Aylesworth. *Upper Atlantic—New Jersey, New York*. New York: Chelsea House, 1987.

Knopf, Alfred. *New York*. New York: Random House, 1995.

The World Almanac and Book of Facts 1999. Ed. Robert Famighetti. New Jersey: Primedia, 1998.

Web Sites

You can also go online and have a look at the following Web sites:

The Official New York State Site
www.iloveny.state.ny.us

New York City Tourism
www.nyctourist.com

New York State Kid's Page
www.oag.state.ny.us/family/kids/kids.html

Some Web sites stay current longer than others. To find other New York Web sites, enter search terms such as "Albany," "New York City," "New Netherland," or any other topic you want to research.

GLOSSARY

abstract expressionism: an artistic style that developed in the 1930s using bold and unusual brush strokes, including paint splattering and solid fields of color

archeological: having to do with the study of ancient artifacts

boroughs: incorporated municipalities smaller than a city

coniferous: evergreen trees and shrubs

deciduous: trees that shed their leaves annually

dissenters: people who depart from an established church or political party

exported: shipped or otherwise transported to another country

hydroelectric power: electricity generated by moving water

inauguration: a formal induction into political office

Jesuit: a member of a Roman Catholic religious order established by a Spaniard named Ignatius in 1534

metropolitan area: a large city and its surrounding communities

persecution: harassing or subjecting people to ill-treatment based on their religion, race, or beliefs

pharmaceuticals: medicinal drugs

philanthropist: a person who practices goodwill toward others through charitable acts

pop art: an art movement that was born in New York City in the 1960s that used images borrowed from popular culture, such as soup cans, comic strips, and road signs

prestigious: reputable

reservations: lands reserved for Native Americans

INDEX